FURNITURE
FACELIFTS

INNOVATIVE WAYS TO GIVE NEW LIFE TO TIRED FURNITURE **SARAH EPTON**

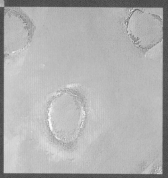

FURNITURE
FACELIFTS

INNOVATIVE WAYS TO GIVE NEW LIFE TO TIRED FURNITURE **SARAH EPTON**

LifeStyle

Publisher: Lisa Simpson • Designer: Emily Cook

This edition first published in Great Britain in 2000 by
LifeStyle
An imprint of Parkgate Books
London House, Great Eastern Wharf, Parkgate Road, London SW11 4NQ

Projects featured in this book have previously appeared in Simply Paint, Simply Stencilling, Simply Fabric, Simply Colour and
Simply Paper by Linda Barker. Published by Anaya. Additional text supplied by Sarah Epton.

© Parkgate Books
A Division of Collins and Brown

A CIP catalogue record for this book is available from the British Library.

ISBN 1-902617-07-X

PRINTED AND BOUND IN CHINA

CONTENTS

5

FURNITURE **FACELIFTS**

INTRODUCTION

All too often, when decorating, we are held back from choosing a particular style or colour for a room because of existing pieces of furniture not fitting into the new scheme of things. It is a common decorating dilemma, however there are many ways to breathe new life into tired furniture and once you have mastered the basic techniques, you can transform a range of old, unsightly or distressed furniture into attractive and functional pieces.

This book challenges the idea that you should throw away all your old bits and pieces to make way for new. Instead it offers a practical and inexpensive alternative, showing you how to make the most of your old chairs, tables, cabinets, wardrobes, chests of drawers, even lampshades. The projects inspire you to create beautiful pieces of furniture from objects that you thought you would never want to see again. By using the following projects as a guide, you can adapt and alter the designs, materials and colour schemes to meet the requirements of your own living environment. The finished creations will be unique to you as an individual and reflect your own distinctive personality, adding both character and style to your home in the process.

When renovating your own furniture, the trick is to treat it as a relaxing hobby and not as a chore. It is important to experiment with different colours and effects, as this is the only way that you will gain confidence and if you make a mistake it isn't the end of the world, in most cases you can simply

paint over it and start again. Learning the various techniques does take time and patience but it will become easier with practice and obviously all your hard work and effort is rewarded in the end when you can stand back and view the finished article in your home, knowing that you created it.

There are very few rules and regulations to follow when it comes to furniture decoration as most of it is down to personal taste and self-expression, however there are several helpful hints and tips that you should be aware of.

- Make sure that you have the correct equipment. It is always worth spending a little bit extra on tools and materials that will be long-lasting, safe and reliable.

- Protect your work surfaces. If you can't afford professional dust sheets you can use newspaper, scrap paper, plastic bags, dustbin liners, and even old bed linen, which is perfect if the area you are working on is particularly large.

- When using paint or other intoxicating substances, always work in a well-ventilated room and take regular breaks in the fresh air.

- Make sure the piece of furniture that you are working on is well prepared. In most cases, the surface will need to be sanded down and sealed with a primer before any decorative detail is applied.

- Seal and protect your finished work with a few coats of varnish – this isn't absolutely necessary but it does help painted surfaces survive the wear and tear of everyday family life.

PROJECTS

PAINTED CHAIR

1 If your chair is neutral in colour and is relatively free of old paint effects and varnishes, then it will not require extensive preparation. However, there is possibility that your chair will previously have been painted and it is important to remove this before applying any new products. To prepare the chair, rub the entire surface with course grade sandpaper, which will remove any old paint and impurities, then finish with fine grade paper to ensure you are left with a smooth surface.

MATERIALS

White acrylic primer

Coloured emulsion

White emulsion

Household paint brush

Sandpaper

Paint kettle

Newspaper/protective sheet

2 After the chair has been sanded down, use a household paint brush to apply the primer. You may find it easier to turn the chair upside down and paint the underside and legs first, then once this has started to dry, you can place the chair in the correct position (preferably on newspaper or a protective sheet) and paint the rest. It should only need one coat.

3 Allow the primer to dry completely, then apply the top coat to the entire chair. In the picture on the previous page, each chair has been painted a different shade of blue. This effect is achieved using the same blue emulsion paint, poured into a paint kettle and gradually mixed with increasing quantities of white emulsion. Leave to dry and varnish to protect if desired.

NEWSPAPER GLAZE

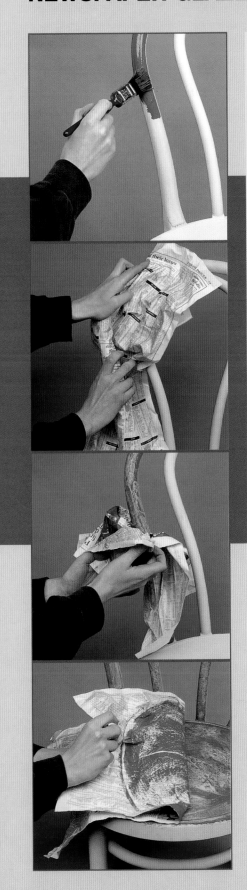

1 Sand the chair down to a smooth finish. Prepare with a layer of white acrylic primer and leave to dry. Pour some of the coloured emulsion top coat into a paint kettle and gently add the white emulsion a little at a time to make the base coat. Blend the mixture together until you obtain a notably lighter shade of the original colour. Apply this to the chair and allow to dry thoroughly. Next, add the top coat to a very small area of the frame.

2 Loosely crumple some newspaper and apply to the freshly painted area – for this effect to work, the top coat needs to remain slightly wet or tacky. Dab gently with the newspaper in order to remove some of the paint but try to avoid rubbing too harshly, as this will remove too much of the colour and ruin the overall effect.

3 Leave the newspaper wrapped around the area for a few seconds to absorb some of the excess paint, then carefully remove to reveal the desired pattern. If you are happy with the effect, repeat the process, a stage at a time, around the entire chair. Once you have completed some of the framework in this way, you will become more confident and will probably be able to increase the size of the areas that you are working on.

4 The seat of the chair should be approached in exactly the same way as before – simply apply a layer of top coat, lay the crumpled newspaper across the surface, press slightly and then peel away gently. Once the newspaper effect is complete, you can varnish the chair to seal and protect if you so wish.

MATERIALS FOR NEWSPAPER GLAZE EFFECT

White acrylic primer • Coloured emulsion paint – top coat

White emulsion paint • Household paint brush

Paint kettle • Newspaper • Sandpaper

FURNITURE **FACELIFTS**

COLOUR-RUBBED LINEN BASKET

1 Using a narrow long haired brush, base-coat the linen basket with the white acrylic primer. Try to push the paint right into the basket weave – you can cut corners and use a spray-on acrylic primer if you haven't got the time to do this. Clean your brush, and when the base coat is completely dry, apply the coloured emulsion. It doesn't matter if the paint seeps through the basket as you can always line the inside afterwards.

14

MATERIALS

Scallop shells

White acrylic primer

Coloured emulsion paint

Medium grade wire wool

Fine grade sandpaper

Long haired brush

Paint brush

Paint kettle

Cotton cloth

Newspaper

All-purpose adhesive

2 Following the weave of the basket, carefully rub away patches of the paint with wire wool. Use enough pressure to remove the paint but try not to press too hard, as you don't want the wicker to show through. Dust away any remaining pieces of wire wool with a paint brush. If the basket needs highlighting, you could add some specs of white emulsion onto the raised parts of the basket; simply dip the tip of a dry brush into the emulsion and lightly flick your wrist to transfer the paint.

3 Dilute the coloured emulsion with 50% water in a paint kettle, then place the shells on newspaper. If the edges of the shells are a little sharp, rub them gently with sandpaper, and then carefully apply the paint. Once dry, rub the shells firmly with a dry cotton cloth, which will remove most of the colour and allow the natural markings of the shell to show through. Using a strong adhesive, secure the shells onto the lid of the basket.

HINT

If your bathroom is particularly humid, you could use oil instead of water-based paints, however this will have to be diluted with white spirit.

FURNITURE **FACELIFTS**

LEAFY TABLE TOP

1 Using an electronic sander or coarse grade sandpaper, strip the table of any old varnish or paint. Once the table is prepared, you can make the stencil. Trace your leaf shape onto cardboard and cut around the outline with a craft knife, then holding your stencil carefully in place, paint masking fluid though your stencil using an old paint brush. Repeat this process until you have an informal leaf pattern across the tabletop.

MATERIALS

Table

Sander and sandpaper (coarse, medium and fine grades)

Thin cardboard

Craft knife

Old paint brush

Masking fluid

Paint brushes

Green emulsion paint

Artist's paint brush

Pink acrylic paint

Grey acrylic paint

Furniture wax

2 Paint over the surface of the table with the green emulsion paint, bearing in mind, that the table will later be distressed so don't worry about trying to achieve a flawless finish. Neither should you worry if you paint over the leaf shapes, as the dried masking fluid will still be visible through the paint. Once the emulsion is quite dry, you can peel off the leaves. If, at first, this proves difficult, try rubbing the surface of the masking fluid with your finger which will soon cause it to wrinkle. To distress the tabletop, sand it down using medium then fine grade sandpaper.

3 Paint the leaves with thick strokes of pink acrylic paint using a fairly broad artist's brush, then apply the grey paint in quick strokes to create the veined leaf detail. Finally, when the paint is quite dry, coat the whole of the table top with a layer of antique wax which will seal and protect the surface.

HINT

During the application of the masking fluid, which is excellent for creating this sort of decorative detail, you should wash the brush regularly in warm soapy water to prevent a build-up; otherwise it may clog up your brush.

FURNITURE **FACELIFTS**

LEAF TEMPLATES

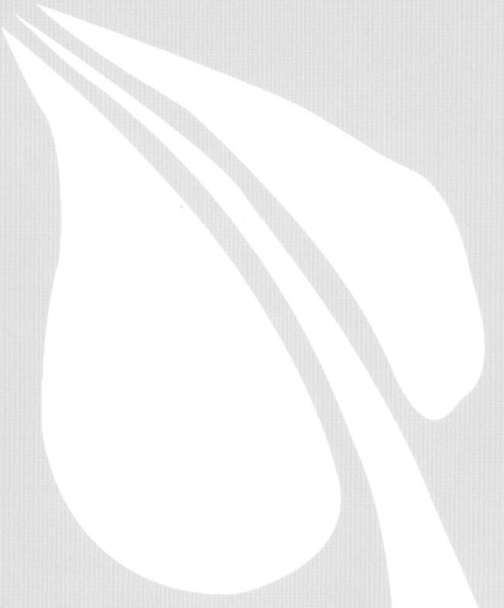

TIE-ON CHAIR COVER

1 From the pattern paper, cut three main pieces; one long piece which should run from the front hem all the way over the seat and backrest to the back hem, and two side pieces. Then, using the paper pattern as a template, cut out the fabric, adding 1.25cm/½in onto all sides for the seam allowance.

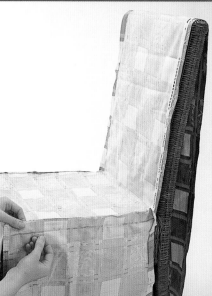

MATERIALS
Pattern paper

Fabric

Scissors

Fusible webbing

Pins

Thread

Needle

Ribbons

2 Set the cover on the chair inside out, then, along the sides that are not sewn, neatly fold over the seam allowance and press flat with an iron. Sew, or if time is short, use fusible webbing on the seams. Next, pin and sew the two side pieces to the seat and front edges – bear in mind these are the only two seams to be sewn together.

3 Turn the cover over and stitch pairs of ribbons along the length of the open seams. You can add as many ribbons as you like but you need to make sure they are placed opposite each other. Finally, tie the ribbons into neat bows and trim the ends to create a pleasant finishing touch.

HINT

Fusible webbing can be used as an alternative to sewing. You can turn up the seams and secure the ribbons in this way, but it needs to be pointed out that it is not particularly hardwearing and therefore, may not survive the washing machine.

HINT

It is often worthwhile, when working on larger objects, to rub some hard wax between the layers of emulsion. This will enable you to remove the top coat from the base coat with a minimum of effort.

SPICE RACK

1 Begin by applying a base coat to the spice rack. If you have chosen a pink and blue colour scheme, similar to that shown here, use pink emulsion for the base. However, if you are using different colours, follow the same principle and add the strongest colour first. Apply the base coat with a small paint brush, which will enable you to reach into the corners and achieve good, accurate coverage. Once the base coat is dry, add a layer of the blue paint, although don't worry about creating such a flawless finish this time as most of it will later be removed.

2 Allow the blue top coat to dry, then take a piece of medium grade sandpaper and gently rub the surface of the spice rack. Areas of pink emulsion will begin to appear from underneath the blue layer. Try applying more pressure to certain areas, which will reveal more of the base coat, and eventually some of the natural wood may even show through. This creates a very effective distressed finish, perfect for any country kitchen.

MATERIALS

Plain spice rack

Pink emulsion paint

Blue emulsion paint

Small paint brushes

Medium grade sandpaper

FURNITURE **FACELIFTS**

DECORATED DRAWERS

Firstly, collect the pictures that you wish to use to decorate the drawers. Here, we use birds, however it is entirely up to you as to what theme you chose (see 'hints'). You need only cover the front panels, but it is always a good idea to cut out more images than you think you will need so you can put together a collage.

24

MATERIALS

Coloured pictures

Craft knife

Painted drawers

PVA glue

Watercolour paint

White emulsion paint

Household paint brush

Wire wool

2

Once you have chosen your pictures, carefully cut them out with a craft knife. Assemble them on the drawer panels – it may be easier to remove the drawer knobs first – moving them around until you are satisfied with the arrangement. When the design is complete, use PVA to glue the images firmly in place.

3

In order to make the images blend with the painted surface of the drawers, slowly mix a little watercolour paint with white emulsion until you form a colour similar to that on the drawers – it doesn't have to be exact. Apply this sparingly over the pictures, then using wire wool, rub away some of the wet paint, this will distress it slightly, adding further detail.

HINT

You may wish to use images that represent the contents of the drawers, perhaps make-up or jewellery for the dressing room, cooking utensils for the kitchen, or toys for the playroom. Not only is this a nice touch, it will also help you to remember what it is you are storing!

KITCHEN WALL CABINET

1 Attach the stencil to the door using repositioning spray and beginning with the four corner leaves, work your way around the frame. You may find it easier to complete the two longer side edges next, then move on to the top and bottom edges, however this is only a suggestion, and with practice, you will find a method that works best for you. Try to finish with a complete vine leaf.

MATERIALS

Cabinet

Repositioning spray

Stencil

Stencil paints

Stencil brush

Palette

Scrap paper

Medium grade sandpaper

Varnish

Household brush

2 Using the registration marks of the previously stencilled image, apply the second overlay. Remember that after dipping your stencil brush into the second colour, you will need to transfer any excess paint onto a piece of scrap paper, newspaper or kitchen roll; otherwise you may be left with unsightly blotches and splashes.

3 As a finishing touch, it is important to make the stencil appear as if it has always been a part of the surface that you are working on. For instance, the cupboard in this project is already distressed, therefore the stencil looks too new. If this is the case, gently rub over the surface of the image with sandpaper until it blends with the rest of the cupboard. Finish by applying two coats of varnish to seal your design.

HINT

Water-based stencil paints
will not work on all surfaces.
If your cupboard has a
melamine or plastic finish,
you will need to use oil-based
paints instead

FURNITURE **FACELIFTS**

RUBBED CHAIR

1 To prepare the chair, rub down with sandpaper until any old paint has been removed and you are left with a smooth finish. If you feel that priming is necessary, you must do this first, then apply the base colour. Generally, a strong base colour is most effective as it needs to be bold enough to show through once the top coat has been applied and rubbed.

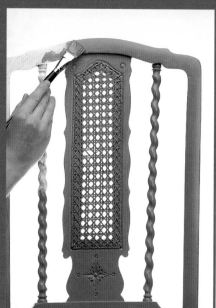
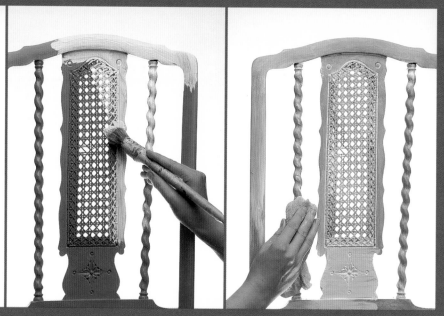

MATERIALS

**Coloured oil-based paint
– base coat**

**White oil-based paint
– top coat**

Transparent oil glaze

Paint brush

Cotton cloth

White spirit

Paint kettle

Sandpaper

2 Once the base colour is thoroughly dry, you can apply the top coat. In a paint kettle, mix together equal quantities of the white oil-based paint and oil glaze. Apply the mixture evenly to the chair – or whatever your chosen piece of furniture is – and allow to dry a little.

3 Your top coat need only be partly dry before you start to remove it. The most effective way to do this is to take a cotton cloth, folded into a smooth pad, and gently rub off the glaze using a light stroking motion. The base colour will gradually start to show through and you may notice that some of the glaze is held in recesses or carvings. This creates a particularly distinctive finish.

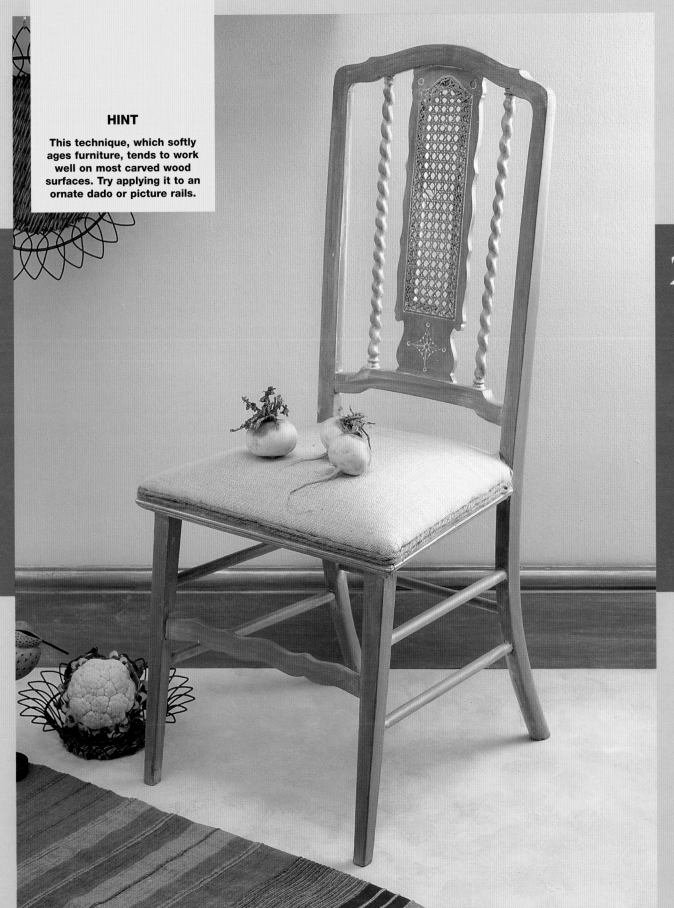

HINT

This technique, which softly ages furniture, tends to work well on most carved wood surfaces. Try applying it to an ornate dado or picture rails.

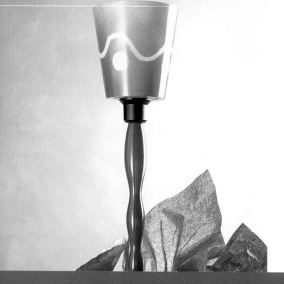

SPRAY PAINT LAMPSHADE

1 Firstly, decide what sort of design you would like to see on your lampshade. If you have opted for the wave pattern, remove the shade from the lamp, decide where you wish your wavy line to run and determine the circumference with a tape measure. The positioning of the wave is important; for instance, it will be emphasized if placed near the base of the shade where the shading is darker.

MATERIALS

Lamp

Cloth tape measure

Self-adhesive plastic

Marker pen

Scissors

Spray paint

2 Taking the circumference as the length, and the depth of the wave as the width, cut a rectangle from the self-adhesive plastic. Use the marker pen to draw a continuous wavy line across the length of the rectangle, trying to maintain an equal distance between each of the crests. Next, cut enough small shapes from a separate piece of plastic (they don't have to be circles) to fit beneath each wave.

3 Once you have cut the wave from the plastic sheet, leaving a width of 1cm/2.5in, remove the backing paper and stick it onto the lampshade. Try to position the wave so that it is flat and level all the way around; otherwise the spray paint may seep through under the adhesive tape and ruin your design. Finally, position the shapes and spray the entire shade (see 'Hints'). Leave to dry before carefully removing the plastic.

HINT

In order to achieve a finely graduated paint finish, place the bottom part of the lampshade nearest the spray paint nozzle. This means that it will receive more paint than the top part of the shade and therefore be darker in colour. The result is very effective.

FURNITURE **FACELIFTS**

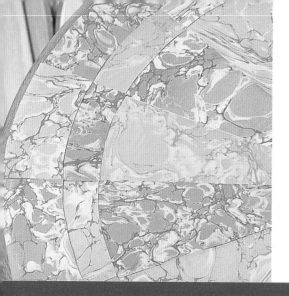

MARBLED TABLE TOP

1 Firstly, you need to make a template from which all your marbled paper pieces will be measured. To do this, tape a sheet of thin paper to the table top and draw around the circumference as accurately as you can, then cut it out with a sharp knife. Fold the circle in half repeatedly until there are sixteen segments. Cut out one of the segments to use as your template.

MATERIALS

Table

Thin paper for template

Pencil

Craft knife

Scissors

Four colours of marbled paper

Tape measure

PVA glue

Varnish

2 Using your template, cut out a total of sixteen segments from each of the coloured marble papers. Once you have completed this, use a pencil to mark off two sections at the top of the original template, approximately 5cm/2in apart, then cut them out. Now, using these, section the marbled paper segments in exactly the same way as the original.

3 Draw a line across the diameter of the table, then using the tape measure, divide the table top into sixteen segments. Once you are satisfied that you have equal sized sections, use the PVA to glue the marbled paper pieces firmly onto the table. It is entirely up to you as to how you arrange the segments but a pattern such as the one shown here, where the colours are alternating, works well. Finally, apply four coats of varnish to seal and protect.

HINT

When cutting out the paper segments for this project, it would be worthwhile to lay down newspaper in order to protect the surface of the table.

FURNITURE **FACELIFTS**

SUNFLOWER DIRECTOR'S CHAIR

1 Place your stencil onto the fabric and fix with a little repositioning spray. Apply colour first to the centre of the sunflower and work your way out. You will notice that large borders do not separate the areas of colour so it would be wise to work with a blunt-edged artist's brush to avoid overlapping the colours. Paint the leaves using a similar brush. Try to use two shades of green to create a more interesting effect.

MATERIALS

Director's chair

Tape measure

Repositioning spray

Stencil

Fabric paints

Metallic/pearlised paints

Artist's brushes

Palette

2 When the sunflower is complete, you can begin painting the other motifs. Here, I have used metallic gold paint for the sun motif to create a glowing effect, this is complemented by an attractive pearlised colour which I have chosen for the criss-cross detail. Feel free to experiment with various colours and textures as stencil paints are very versatile and mixing them often adds character to a design

3 When the first line of colour is complete, carefully remove the stencil, however, try to avoid lifting the acetate before all the paint has been applied; otherwise the edges of the pattern will not stay sharp. Line up the registration marks with the previously stencilled areas and begin the next line, you may need to use a little more repositioning spray. Repeat steps 1 and 2.

HINT

Try to envisage how you would like your design to look, then carefully position your first stencil. The aim is to avoid stencilling any incomplete sunflowers into the design.

FURNITURE **FACELIFTS**

FLOWER AND FRUIT TEMPLATES

36

FURNITURE **FACELIFTS**

STENCILLED DRAWERS

1 If you are working with a new, unpainted piece of furniture, you should not need a base coat, however older surfaces may need more preparatory work before you start to decorate them. Prepare your chest of drawers with white acrylic primer and allow to dry. Paint the framework with coloured emulsion paint.

MATERIALS

White acrylic primer

**2 coloured emulsion paints –
top coats**

Pre-cut stencil

Stencil brush

Spray adhesive

Paint for stencil

Paint brush

Saucer

Scrap paper

2 You may wish to paint a panel onto the front of the drawers, which will certainly add character and individuality to your design. Here, we have used pale to mid tones, creating a more sophisticated look for an adult environment, but of coarse, for a child's room, bright and stimulating primary colours are much more suitable.

3 Pour a small amount of stencil paint onto a saucer, then position the pre-cut stencil onto an area of the drawer with a little spray adhesive or repositioning spray. This will be your starting point. Dip the stencil brush into the paint and dab off any excess onto scrap paper. Using a circular motion of the brush, carefully apply the paint to the stencil and work your way across the chest until your design is complete.

HINT

When stencilling, always use your paint sparingly and try blending a slightly lighter or darker shade over the first colour, this creates a more subtle effect.

DESIGN TEMPLATES

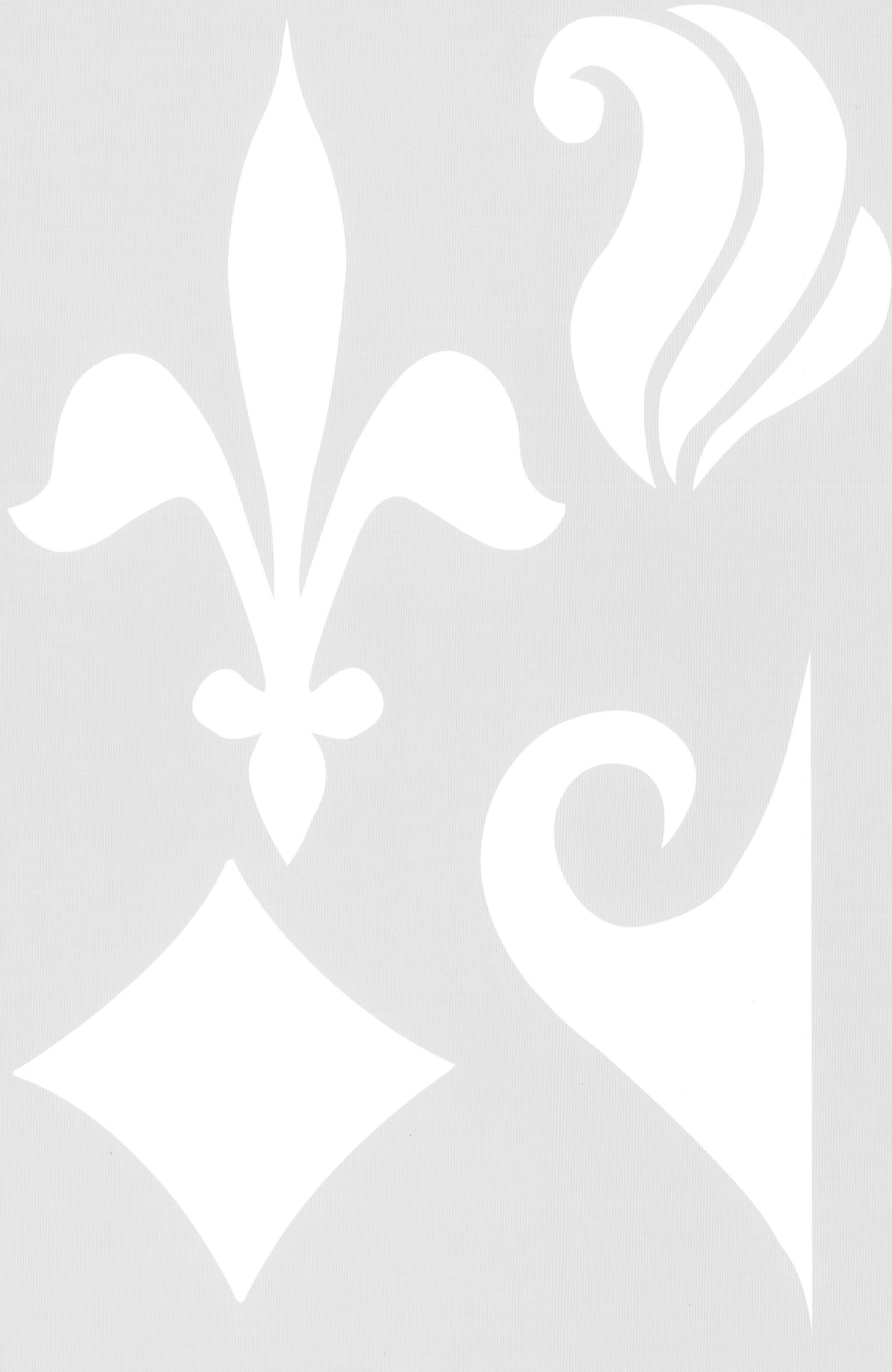

CUSHION COVER

1 Design your stencil, then using a photocopier, enlarge the image to 30cm/12in square. Evenly spray the back of the photocopy with repositioning spray and affix the design firmly to the manila card. Carefully cut out the design using a set square and a craft knife; remember that you will be cutting through both the photocopy and the card so you will need to apply substantial pressure. Always work on a cutting board.

MATERIALS

Black and white image

Manila card

Repositioning spray

Set square

Craft knife

Cutting board

Cushion cover

Masking tape

Scrap paper for masking

Car spray paints

2 Position the manilla stencil onto the flat cushion cover. Secure it to the fabric with repositioning spray. Protect the areas that you do not wish to paint by covering the surrounding area with scrap paper and masking tape, this is important, as spray paint will inevitably drift. It would also be wise to place a sheet of card inside the cushion cover to prevent paint seeping through to the back.

3 Apply the spray paint to the fabric in a series of short blasts. Use as many colours as you wish and try to gradually build up interesting shading effects. In this particular project, three colours have been used beginning with the lightest in the centre of the design encircled by increasingly darker shades.

HINT

For larger and more open stencils such as this, it is advisable to use manilla card as opposed to acetate. The reason being that it is more rigid and easier to handle on objects with greater surface areas.

FURNITURE **FACELIFTS**

PATTERN TEMPLATES

FURNITURE **FACELIFTS**

LIMEWASHED CUPBOARD

1 Using a sanding block, remove any unwelcome traces of dirt and grease from the surface of the wood. Begin this process with medium grade sandpaper and finish off with fine grade. Next, apply masking tape to the inside of the frame, which will protect the surfaces that are not to be painted from any stray splashes of paint. It will also help to create a neat finish providing you peel it away carefully.

MATERIALS

White emulsion paint

5cm/2in paint brush

Paint kettle

Cotton cloth

Masking tape

Medium/coarse grade wire wool

Sanding block

Medium/fine grade sandpaper

2 As I am sure you are aware, different woods have different textures, which means that the amount of paint required will vary according to the porosity of the wood. To test this, dilute some emulsion paint with water in a paint kettle and apply a little of the mixture to the wood. The consistency is at the right level when the wood grain is still clearly visible through the layer of paint. Apply the emulsion, gradually in small workable sections.

3 Whilst the paint is still wet, take a cotton cloth and rub the emulsion into the wood until you are left with a feint veil of white over the surface and thicker streaks of white running through the grains in the wood. Finally, gently sand down the wood with fine grade sandpaper to create a distressed effect.

HINT

Always work in the direction of the wood grain. It is also useful to bear in mind that new wood tends not to be very porous, therefore it may help to prepare it with medium/coarse grade wire wool which will scratch the surface and enable it to hold the paint better.

HINT

As you are using an oil-based paint for this project, it is advisable to use only plastic or acetate from which to cut your stencils, anything else, such as cardboard, may absorb the paint and ruin the sharpness of the design.

FISH BATHROOM CABINET

1 This technique is known as a reverse stencil whereby the fishes will register as clear against the frost-effect glass. Firstly, trace simple fish shapes directly onto the plastic or acetate – use a marker pen if the pencil is not legible. Carefully cut around the shapes with a craft knife and use repositioning spray to stick each of them on the reverse of the glass door.

2 Mix together some of the white oil-based paint with an equal quantity of the polyurethane varnish. Dip your stencil brush into the mixture, which will be quite fluid, and work off any excess paint onto scrap paper, then stipple over the glass. Leave the paint to dry thoroughly before attempting to remove the fish, as it is very easy to scratch the stippled surface. Once you are satisfied the paint is dry, carefully remove the fish shapes. The simplest way to do this is to peel them off with tweezers or the tip of your craft knife. A steady hand is required!

MATERIALS

Thick plastic or acetate sheet

Marker pen or pencil

Craft knife

Repositioning spray

Cabinet

White oil-based paint

Polyurethane varnish

Palette

Stencil brush

Scrap paper

Tweezers

FURNITURE **FACELIFTS**

MARINE TEMPLATES

STENCILLED LARDER CUPBOARD

1 First, prime the cupboard, then apply two layers of emulsion base coat. Rub each dry layer with sandpaper before applying the next for the smoothest possible surface. Next, cut a piece of cartridge paper to fit the cupboard door panel and using a pencil and ruler, divide the paper into 5cm/2in squares. At the corners of each square, where the lines cross, draw a leaf shape.

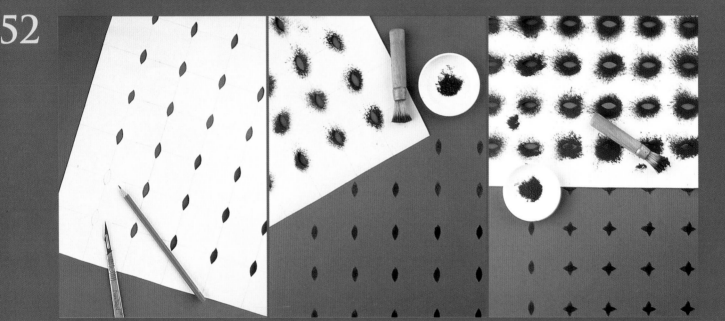

MATERIALS

White acrylic primer

**Coloured emulsion paint –
base coat**

Coloured emulsion paint for stencil

Cartridge paper

Craft knife

Stencil brush

Sandpaper

Pencil

Ruler

Masking tape

Newspapers

2 After carefully cutting out your leaf shapes with a craft knife, affix the stencil to the door panel with masking tape. Using a stencil brush, paint through the leaf pattern stencil with the second coloured emulsion. When this part of the design is complete, slowly peel away the masking tape, taking care not to remove any of the base colour.

3 Reposition the stencil by turning it through 90 degrees so that the leaf shapes now lie horizontally across those already stencilled. Secure the cartridge paper in the new position with masking tape and again, stencil the leaf shape onto the door panel using the same coloured emulsion.

HINT

Not only is stencilling a great way to decorate your home, it also provides an opportunity to make use of all your left over emulsion. Alternatively, you could buy inexpensive sample pots of colour or test the wide range of stencil paints now available.

FURNITURE **FACELIFTS**

WOODSTAINED TABLE

1 Using a tape measure, determine the depth of the border, and mark off the area with masking tape. Next, mark the centre point of each internal edge with a pencil then, using masking tape, join the marks together to create the centre diamond shape. Score along all of the inside edges within the taped areas with a ruler and craft knife, this prevents the stains from bleeding across the grain. Next, apply the first colour to the centre of the diamond, making sure you stay within the confines of the tape.

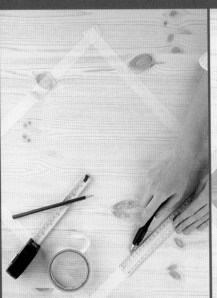

MATERIALS

Coffee table

Tape measure

Masking tape

Craft knife

Ruler

3 coloured woodstains

Saucers

Paint brushes

Furniture wax

2 Allow the first colour to dry for a few minutes, then remove the masking tape. To apply the second colour, place masking tape, once again, around the edges of the diamond but this time the outside edge of the tape should rest on the edge of the stain and the scored line. You should notice four triangular shapes appear between the diamond and the border, paint these with the second colour.

3 Divide the length of the border into squares, ensuring that you have the same amount on each side but that each side contains an uneven number. Section off every other square with masking tape and score the table in the usual way. Apply the third colour and leave to dry. Then, as before, mask off the painted squares, which will enable you to paint the remaining chequers with the first colour. Stain the rest of the table with a single colour and protect with wax if necessary.

HINT

This pattern is designed with a square table in mind but it can be varied to suit a different shaped table. Also, it is useful to know that woodstain should always be applied to unfinished wood so that the pigment is absorbed. If you are using an old table, ensure it is stripped and sanded before starting.

55

FURNITURE **FACELIFTS**

PAINTED CUPBOARD

1 Firstly, before you begin working on the leaf design, prepare the cupboard with primer, leave to dry, then apply the base colour. Next, draw a simple leaf shape onto cardboard and cut around it with scissors to make a template. Wait until the base coat is thoroughly dry then, using the template and a pencil, randomly cover the cupboard with leaves, and paint them with a strong coloured emulsion.

MATERIALS

White acrylic primer

Coloured emulsion paint – base coat

3 Coloured emulsion paints – for leaf design

Fine artist's brush

Paint brush

Thin cardboard

Pencil

Scissors

2 Using exactly the same method as before, draw an oak leaf shape, which will sit in the centre of the first leaf. Draw the shape onto cardboard and cut it out to make a template. Check that the paint on the original leaf is dry and if so, position the new template within, then draw around it. Paint with a lighter shade of emulsion so that it stands out against the colour of the original leaf shape.

3 When the second part of the pattern is quite dry, use a contrasting colour to add an easy finishing touch to your design. Simply take a fine artist's brush, dip it into the third colour and paint a series of single curved lines onto the cupboard in the spaces between the leaves. Create the lines with a quick sweeping freehand movement of the brush.

HINT

If you wish, use the pattern here as a guideline. You don't have to follow it exactly as any simple stylised leaf shape will work. Experiment with various leaf shapes before you commit to one particular design.

VEGETABLE PRINTED TABLE

1 Firstly, sand and prime the table top, then apply a coat of white emulsion to the whole table and allow to dry. With the coloured emulsion paint the legs of the table, leaving the table top white. Once the legs are dry you can start work on the table top. Using a pencil and ruler, divide the surface of the table into 15cm/6in squares. Don't panic if the table top is uneven, the design is perfect for a country setting and this will simply add to the effect.

MATERIALS

White acrylic primer

**White emulsion paint –
base coat**

**Coloured emulsion paint –
printing**

Potato

Knife

Sandpaper

Felt tipped pen

Pencil

Ruler

Saucer

Newspaper

2 It is probably best to start painting in the outlines of the squares first, creating the tiled effect. Cut a large potato in half lengthways and draw a long, single bar on the surface of one half of the potato with felt tipped pen. Cut out and remove the excess pieces of potato surrounding the bar so that the shape stands proud. Pour a little of the emulsion paint into a saucer, dip the bar into the paint and print onto the table using your pencil outlines as a guide.

3 Draw a second pattern for the centre of the tiles onto the remaining potato half, then as before, use a sharp knife to cut around the pattern and remove the excess potato. Dip the potato into the paint and apply to the tiles. For both the outline and the centre design, it would be advisable to test the pattern on a sheet of newspaper first, this allows you to see how the finished effect will look and also gets rid of excess paint, which may smudge and ruin your design.

HINT

You may find that as your design begins to take shape, the potato becomes quite slippery. You can deal with this problem by sticking a fork into its back and creating a handle, or by simply wearing rubber gloves for a better grip.

COVERED FOOTSTOOL

1 Cut both coloured fabrics to fit over, around and just underneath the footstool. Both pieces should be of equal size. Baste the fabrics together. Next, create a template, and remember if your original shape is too small, you can always enlarge it on a photocopier. Using the chalk and the template, draw stars at random around the surface of the fabric, avoiding the edges.

MATERIALS

Scissors

2 pieces of contrasting fabric

Chalk

Pins

Sewing machine

Thread

Staple gun

Tacks

Hammer

Hessian

Template

2 Position pins at various points around the stars to hold them in place. Take a coloured thread, preferably one that contrasts with the fabrics, and using a sewing machine, thread a close zig-zag stitch around the chalk outlines. Once the seams are secure, carefully cut around the inside of the sewn areas with scissors. Ensure that you only remove the top layer and try to avoid piercing the fabric underneath.

3 Lay the fabric upside down on a flat surface and place the footstool on top. Pull the fabric tightly up and over the sides, fixing to the underside of the stool with staples. Make neat mitred folds at each corner and secure in the same way. Attach a piece of hessian to the underside of the stool to cover the staples and secure with carpet tacks. If necessary, paint the legs to match the cover, and reassemble.

HINT

If at all possible, remove the legs when measuring the fabric to fit around the stool. This makes the job a whole lot easier and you will achieve a far greater level of accuracy.

STAR AND MOON TEMPLATES

FURNITURE **FACELIFTS**

GILDED TABLE TOP

1 Firstly, clean the glass top to remove any grease and impurities, and place upside down on protective paper. Select a number of leaves and arrange these on the glass top, use various shapes and sizes to create a more interesting pattern. Manoeuvre the leaves into different positions until you are satisfied with the design.

MATERIALS

Glass table top

Leaves

Blu-tack

Protective paper

Spray varnish

Dutch metal leaf

Household brush

2 Affix the leaves onto the glass; use blu-tack for this as it allows you to reposition the leaves if you make a mistake. Place small pieces of blu-tack along each part of the leaf so they will lie as flat as possible on the surface of the glass. This is essential as it prevents the spray varnish from seeping underneath and ruining the effect. Once the leaves are positioned, apply the varnish. Spray evenly from left to right then top to bottom until the entire surface is covered.

3 Wait for the varnish to become slightly tacky. Peel away the leaves and cover the glass top with Dutch metal leaf, ensure the entire surface is covered. After the metal leaf has been applied, gently rub the surface with a small dry brush, the excess will begin to lift from the leaf shapes, which remain dry, as they have not been sprayed with the varnish. Apply another layer of varnish to protect your design.

HINT

It is quite acceptable to substitute the Dutch metal leaf for gold leaf although you should be aware that Dutch leaf is a cheaper alternative, which is also sold in a versatile sheet form. The only disadvantage being that, unlike gold leaf, Dutch leaf must be varnished to prevent tarnishing.

FREEHAND PAINTED SERVER CABINET

1 Sand down the cabinet to a smooth finish, and coat with the primer. When this is dry, paint the surrounding frame with the darker oil-based top coat, and the door panels with the lighter colour. Using the artist's oil colour and brush, paint the tree trunk and branches with sweeping freehand strokes. Then, add the leaf shapes by pressing the bristles of the brush firmly against the surface, and lifting off carefully. They do not need to touch the branches.

MATERIALS

Oil-based primer

**2 Coloured oil-based paints –
top coat**

Coloured artist's oil

Artist's brush

White spirit

Sandpaper

Antiquing wax

Cotton cloth

2 Everything about this design is based on simplicity and this includes the bird image, which requires only three basic shapes to suggest its head, body and tail. Pencil in the outlines beforehand if it makes you feel more confident. Finish the design with the small plant detail at the bottom of the tree; apply this in the same way as the branches and the leaves.

3 Allow time for the whole image to dry and then apply a little of the antiquing wax. Use a soft cotton cloth and gently rub over the surface of the cabinet. The end result will be a slightly distressed, aged look which is designed to make newly painted pieces of furniture fit into their surroundings, creating the impression that they have been in your home for years.

HINT

Your subject matter is not only limited to cabinets, this design looks good on anything with a central panel, and is just as easy to apply. You could even try it on panelled internal doors for an interesting and individual look.

ANTIQUED WARDROBE

1 Apply the primer followed by the lighter coloured base coat, sanding down between coats to achieve a smooth finish. Leave to dry, and apply a thin layer of crackle glaze. Only apply the glaze to the panels (if your wardrobe has them), as this will emphasize their shape. Coat with the second coloured emulsion paint, working your way around the framework first. Paint the panels last and be quick, as once the paint and glaze interact, cracks will appear almost immediately.

MATERIALS

White acrylic primer

**Coloured emulsion paint –
base coat**

Crackle glaze

**Coloured emulsion paint –
top coat**

Sanding block

Sandpaper

Wire wool

**Artist's acrylic paint –
burnt umber**

Paint brush

Paint kettle

2 Wait until the final layer is dry before starting the next stage and don't worry if you have achieved a less than perfect finish. Use a sanding block to rub away patches of colour creating the impression of wear and tear. You can determine how little or how much of the paint is removed by varying the degree of pressure applied with the sanding block, and to avoid mistakes, work in stages, stepping back from the project regularly to view the wardrobe in its entirety.

3 When you are satisfied with your design, take a little of the burnt umber artist's paint and dilute with water in a small paint kettle. Dip the wire wool into the mixture and apply sparingly to the wardrobe using a circular rubbing motion. Remember that during this process, you will inevitably remove further patches of paint whilst at the same time, leaving an effective finish.

HINT

Choose a colour scheme that suits your own requirements, however you should always make sure that the base and top coats contrast to create a strong final effect.

FURNITURE **FACELIFTS**

LEMON BORDER TABLE

1 Enlarge the lemon border image on a photocopier – remembering to include the registration marks – until it measures 12.5cm/5in deep. Affix this copy to the back of an acetate sheet using a little repositioning spray and cut out the leaf detail, adding the registration marks for the lemons as you go. Repeat this process on a separate acetate sheet, however this time, cut out the lemons and flowers and mark off the leaves.

MATERIALS

Table

Tracing paper

Ink pen

Stencil sheet

Repositioning spray

Craft knife

Cutting board

Stencil brushes

Stencil paint

Masking tape

Scrap paper

Sandpaper

Varnish

2 Position the first acetate sheet against the edge of the table, secure with repositioning spray and stencil in the leaves using two shades of green. Remove, and apply the other stencil layer, remembering to line up the registration marks, and paint in the fruits and flowers using two shades of yellow. Repeat around all four sides of the table, ignoring the corners for now, checking regularly that the horizontal edge is level.

3 Complete the corners by placing the acetate at an angle and masking off those areas that are not required, then stencil through to the table. Once complete, you can leave your design as it is, to gradually be distressed by everyday wear and tear, or you can create the aged look artificially. Simply rub the table with medium grade sandpaper until you have the desired effect. Varnish to protect.

HINT

In addition to using two shades of green and yellow for the design, you can also create a more natural effect by varying the pressure that you apply when stippling.

SEASHELL CABINET

1 Using sandpaper, prepare the cabinet until it is free of any old paint or varnish, however if you are using a brand new cabinet, you do not have to worry about this. Trace your shell shape onto thin cardboard and carefully cut out the image to create a simple stencil. Using the shell template, randomly cover the cabinet with the image and then position the stencil over each one, filling in the shape with masking fluid.

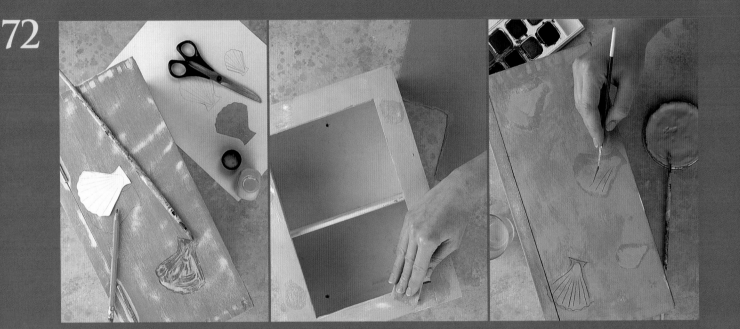

MATERIALS

Bathroom cabinet

Medium and fine grade sandpaper

Thin cardboard

Pencil

Scissors

Masking fluid

Fine paint brush

Coloured emulsion paints

Paint brush

Acrylic varnish

2 Allow the masking fluid to dry then apply a layer of the coloured emulsion to the cabinet. Don't concentrate too much on achieving a flawless finish, some projects, such as this, are made more interesting when you apply the paint in patches so that coverage is uneven. Once the paint is quite dry, peel away the dried masking fluid, revealing the bare wood, and gently rub the surface with sandpaper.

3 Roughly dab the shells with a second coloured emulsion and once again, the emphasis is on patchy – it does not matter if some of the natural wood shows through when the paint dries. Add the shell detail with a fine paint brush, simply draw around the outline, and with a quick flicking movement of the wrist, paint in the centre detail. Apply two layers of acrylic varnish to seal and protect.

HINT

Feel free to experiment with other images associated with marine life, you could try fish shapes or seahorses as an alternative to shells.

KITCHEN STOOL

1 Find a stool that can be taken apart and reassembled easily. Remove all the old seat coverings from the seat base. Cut the gingham into strips of approximately 7.5cm/3in wide and create enough length to cover the seat and have an allowance left over to be stapled underneath. Fold lengthways, and sew a small seam down the side to close each strip.

MATERIALS

Stool

2 colours of gingham

Scissors

Sewing machine

Thread

Staple gun

Oil-based paint

Paint brush

2 Cover the seat base with horizontal strips of fabric, try to pull them as tight as possible otherwise the seat will sag when pressure is applied. Don't worry about the pattern, it can be as random as you wish. This stool, in particular, is already somewhat old and dishevelled so the emphasis is on casual rather than formal. Secure the material with staples underneath the seat base where they cannot be seen.

3 Weave the vertical strips through the horizontal bands, threading them in an 'over one band, under the next' motion. Use whatever colours you want but make sure you alternate the 'over, under' procedure for each strip, the lattice effect created will strengthen the structure. In addition, you will gain even more support by pushing the bands close together. Once you are satisfied with the design, trim the strips underneath the base, paint the stool if necessary and reassemble.

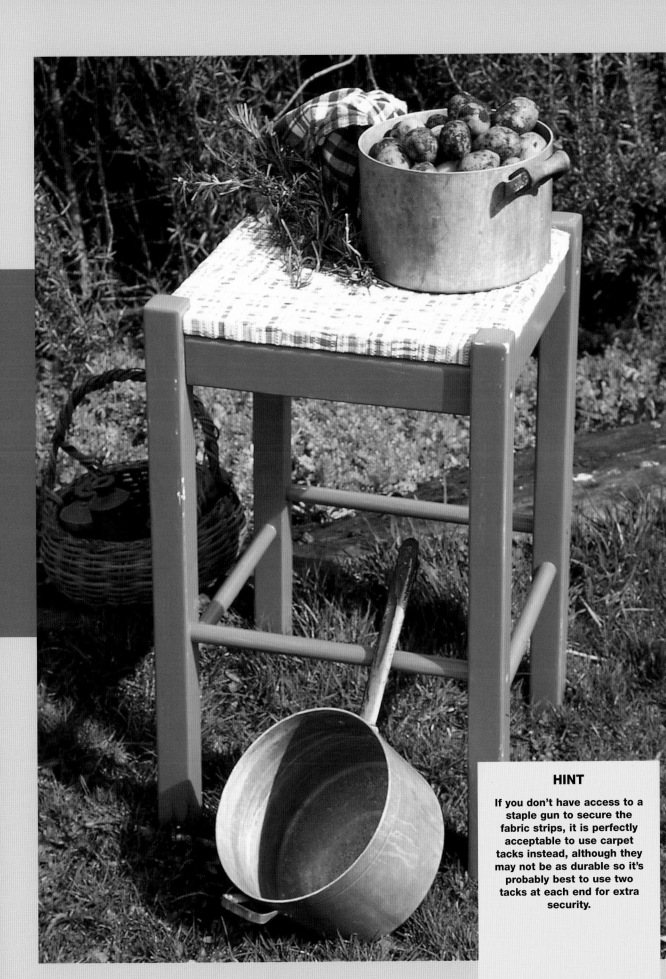

HINT

If you don't have access to a staple gun to secure the fabric strips, it is perfectly acceptable to use carpet tacks instead, although they may not be as durable so it's probably best to use two tacks at each end for extra security.

STAR LAMPSHADE

1 Trace a star shape onto thin paper using a pencil, try to make the pencil lines quite dark in colour so that you will clearly see the outline when placed under the lampshade. Transfer the image onto the lampshade in the same way that you would trace something onto paper. Repeat the design all over the shade, the pattern can be formal, or random like the one shown here.

MATERIALS

Thin paper

Pencil

Lampshade

Craft knife

2 coloured emulsion or water-based paints

Paint brush

Tissue paper

Paper/fabric adhesive

2 Using a sharp craft knife, cut through the fabric around the outlines of the stars and remove the centre. This is quite a painstaking process as the knife could very easily slip off line, therefore you should work very slowly and carefully. Apply a base colour to the shade and leave until quite dry, then splatter the second colour – which should be a little thinner than the first – onto the fabric to create a speckled finish.

3 Take several pieces of coloured tissue paper that are slightly larger than the star images, and using paper or fabric adhesive, glue to the inside of the shade behind each star. Whilst the adhesive is still slightly wet, use the craft knife to cut away the excess paper into a star shape; even though the inside of the shade is somewhat hidden from view, it is important to achieve a tidy finish overall. You will benefit from the full effect of the design when the light is switched on and shines through the stars.

HINT

Emulsion paints are very much suited to this type of project, however if you have access to acrylic or water-based colours, use these instead. The second colour will normally need to be diluted to splatter successfully.

FURNITURE **FACELIFTS**

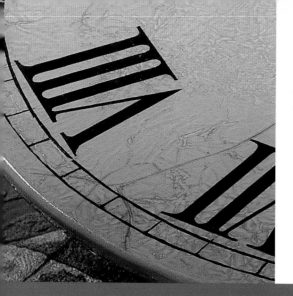

PEN AND INK CLOCK TABLE

1 Prime the surface and leave to dry. Draw on the circular clock face using a pencil tied to one end of a piece of string, with the other end fixed to the centre of the table and pulled taut. This serves as a makeshift compass and allows you to create a perfect circle. The first outline should be about 2.5cm/1in from the edge of the table, and the second the same distance inside the first. In pencil, add the Roman numeral detail – you can either draw them freehand or use the trace and transfer method.

MATERIALS

White oil-based primer

Black waterproof ink

Ink pen and nib

String

Ruler

Pencil

Crackle lure kit (antiquing varnish and water-based varnish)

Artist's oil colour – burnt umber

Cotton cloth

Polyurethane varnish

Paint brush

2 When you are satisfied with your design, paint the numerals and the circular outlines with black ink allowing a little time for this to dry so that it doesn't smudge and ruin your design. Next, using a large household paint brush, coat the whole surface of the table with the antiquing varnish. Wait until this is part dry but still slightly tacky and apply the water-based varnish. Leave until quite dry. During the drying process, hairline cracks will begin to appear forming the basis for your antiqued effect.

3 Roll a soft cotton cloth into a pad and dab on a little of the burnt umber artist's colour. Using gentle circular movements, rub this over the surface of the table and into the cracks. The aim of this process is to define the cracks and enhance the aged appearance of the clock face. When this final layer is completely dry, seal and protect with a coat of polyurethane varnish.

HINT

You can alter the theme of the clock face to suit its surroundings. For instance, if the table were to sit in a child's room, it would perhaps be better to use modern numbers as opposed to Roman numerals.

NUMBER TEMPLATES

12
34
56
78
90

I V X

1 2 3 4 5

IVX

6 7 8 9 0

FURNITURE **FACELIFTS**

HINT

If you have a design for your stencil in mind but the image that you wish to use is the wrong size – perhaps it will not fit on the framework of the chair – you can enlarge or decrease the image using a photocopier.

STENCILLED CHAIR

1 Apply primer and two layers of emulsion base coat in order to prepare the chair for stencilling. Design a motif for the stencil, you can either use the one shown here – which is a perfect fit for the chair legs and frame – or you can choose your own. Using a pencil, or marker pen if the pencil will not register, trace the design directly onto an acetate sheet. Next, cut out the design using a craft knife.

2 Position the stencil on the chair using a little repositioning spray, which will allow you to remove the stencil easily after use. Dip the blunt end of the stencil brush into the paint and dab off the excess onto scrap paper, or any material that will absorb some of the paint such as newspaper or kitchen roll. If you fail to do this, the colour will be too heavy and may run under the bridges of the stencil, as a result you will lose definition and sharpness in the design. Next, stipple the paint through the stencil and allow some time for this to set. Remove the acetate and reposition in such a way that you create a continuous pattern when the colour is applied.

MATERIALS

Chair

Acrylic primer

Emulsion base coat

Household brushes

Pencil

Repositioning spray

Stencil sheet

Cutting board

Craft knife

Stencil brush

Stencil paint

Scrap paper

FURNITURE **FACELIFTS**

HARLEQUIN SEAT COVER

1 Cut a square shaped piece of canvas large enough to fit over and just under the seat base. Fold the square into quarters and press gently to create light creases in the fabric. When you unfold, you will notice a centre point has been marked out where the lines intersect. Trace your diamond pattern onto a stencil sheet and cut out using a craft knife. Place the centre of one of the diamonds over the creased intersection and stipple with fabric paint

MATERIALS

Heavy cotton canvas

Scissors

Craft knife

Stencil sheet

Repositioning spray

Masking tape

Fabric paint

Stencil brush

Cloth

Iron

Staple gun/tacks

2 Carefully reposition the sheet for the next set of diamonds. Registration marks are not used in this particular design so place one row of diamonds on the stencil over a previously stencilled area on the fabric and align in this way until the surface is covered. Patterns such as this can often waver off line if you are not careful when repositioning your stencil. It is easier to start in the centre with a complete diamond and work your way out to the edges – take care not to smudge. Wait until the fabric is completely dry then turn over and iron the underside to fix the paint.

3 Place the fabric over the seat base and staple the excess to the underside, alternatively small tacks would work just as well. When securing the material ensure that it is taut. Place your hands in the centre of the material and smooth outwards to the corners to remove any creases. Tuck each of the corners in neatly and secure. Drop the seat in place, spraying with fabric guard if required.

TRANSFER CIRCULAR TABLE

1 Prepare the table with acrylic primer and then apply the emulsion base coat. Choose a design for your circular table; photocopy an image from a book or draw it freehand if you feel confident enough, and remember that you can always enlarge or decrease the size of the image using a photocopier. Trace the final design using a soft pencil.

2 Place a sheet of transfer paper between the traced image and the table top and carefully reproduce the design. If you have quartered the image, as shown here, place a pin through the tracing and secure it to the centre of the table, this will create a point around which you can rotate your image. When the tracing is complete, apply the artist's acrylic paint.

3 Allow the paint to dry completely. Mix an equal amount of white emulsion paint and glaze in a paint kettle making sure that you blend them well. Remember that you can vary certain aspects of any design and if you do not wish to give your table a faded appearance, simply omit the white emulsion from the mixture. Using an ordinary household paintbrush, apply a thin coat of the mixture to the table top. This layer will seal and protect your design and you will notice that once dry, it creates a subtle faded effect giving the appearance of age.

MATERIALS

White acrylic primer

Emulsion paint – base coat

Artist's acrylic paint

White emulsion paint

Emulsion glaze

Design source book

Transfer paper

Tracing paper

Pencil

Paint brush

Paint kettle

HINT

If you are not satisfied with the original base colour of your pedestal then you can paint it beforehand. However ensure that it is completely dry before you begin the rest of the process and try not to apply too much pressure with the wire brush.

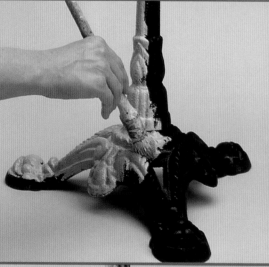

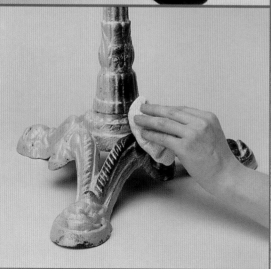

COLOUR-RUBBED PEDESTAL

1 Rub the pedestal with a wire brush in order to prepare for painting. In a paint kettle, mix together equal quantities of the coloured eggshell paint with the glaze and blend well. Apply this, quite liberally, to the pedestal. If your pedestal is heavily carved or contains very deep grooves, you may need to stipple some of the paint into these to ensure that the entire surface is covered.

2 Do not allow the glaze to dry. Almost immediately after application, take a cotton cloth, folded into a smooth pad, and gently wipe away most of the glaze. You need only remove glaze from the surface of the pedestal – the idea being that large areas of the base colour show through but the glaze remains in the carved recesses and grooves to define them.

MATERIALS

Coloured eggshell paint

Transparent oil glaze

Cotton cloth

Wire brush

Fitch brush or soft artist's brush

Paint kettle

Paint brush

FURNITURE FACELIFTS

PAINTED CHAIR

1 To begin, prepare the surface of the chair so it is ready for painting. The level of preparation required depends on the state and age of your chair; for instance, if it contains traces of old paint or varnish, these need to be removed with sandpaper, however if the chair is new you need not worry about this. Using wood glue, position the wood mouldings on the chair and leave to set.

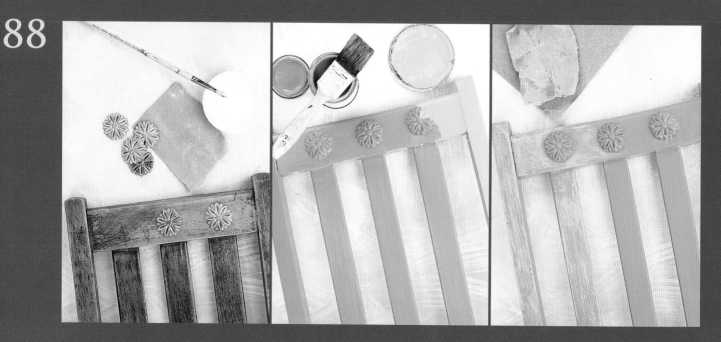

MATERIALS

Chair

Medium grade sandpaper

Wood glue

Glue brush

2 colours of emulsion paint

Paint brush

2 When the wood glue is quite dry, use a household paint brush to apply the top and base coat colours to the chair. You could choose a similar colour scheme to that used here, or you could of course decide to try a more subtle approach. Remember to apply the brightest colour first for a project such as this where distressing is involved and always allow time for the base coat to dry before you apply the second colour.

3 To create the very effective aged look, wear away patches of the top coat to reveal the colour underneath. Do this by gently rubbing the surface with sandpaper, applying a minimum of pressure at first so that you don't remove too much paint, however once you have a feel for it you can vary the amount of colour that you remove. If you do make a mistake and reveal some of the natural wood, simply add a little of the top colour and blend in.

HINT

Junk shops are wonderful places to find sets of old chairs at bargain prices and it would cost very little to decorate an entire set in this way.

89

FURNITURE **FACELIFTS**

SEAT COVER

1 Cut the fabric into eight strips measuring 7.5cm/3in wide and long enough to stretch over and underneath the seat base – it is a good idea to leave plenty of excess, as you may need it later. Using the sewing machine, make two panels, each consisting of four strips alternating in colour. Take one of the panels and divide into twelve smaller strips, each measuring 7.5cm/3in in width. Leave the other panel intact.

MATERIALS

Seat base

2 colours of cotton fabric

Scissors

Sewing machine

Thread

Staple gun

2 Take three of the smaller pieces of fabric and sew them together end to end making one long single strip. Repeat the process, and sew the two new pieces together lengthways to create a chequered panel. Attach this to the original centre panel and repeat on the other side. You should end up with a piece of striped fabric sandwiched between two chequered panels.

3 Place the fabric upside down on a flat surface and lay the seat base on top. Trim off the excess material so that you have just enough to pull over the edges of the seat then, using a staple gun, secure the material to the wooden base. Begin stapling at the centre of each edge and work your way outwards to the corners, smoothing out the creases in the fabric as you go. Neatly fold in the corners and position the seat into the frame of the chair. If you are using expensive material, invest in a spray-on fabric guard which will repel common spills and splashes.

TARTAN DOOR KNOBS

1 Remove the door knobs from the furniture and apply one coat of acrylic primer followed by a layer of emulsion for the base coat – which can be any colour you wish, it does not have to be a neutral shade such as white, beige or cream. The great thing about tartan is that colours can either complement or contrast each other and the surface that they are intended for, therefore the possible combinations are endless.

2 The doorknobs that you are decorating will more than likely be slightly rounded so it may be quite tricky at first to achieve straight lines, therefore It is a good idea to plan your pattern in pencil. You may also find that because of their size, it is difficult to paint doorknobs on a flat surface, in which case you should insert a screw into the base to act as a handle while you paint. Paint over the pencil lines using the coloured emulsion adding horizontal and vertical lines to the surface to produce a chessboard effect.

3 Allow the first colour to dry and then, using a very fine brush, paint sets of double lines through the centre of the chequers both horizontally and vertically. As you work you will notice a very simple but effective tartan pattern beginning to take shape and it is achieved with the minimum of time and effort. Should you wish, you can add to the pattern further but try not to make it appear too cluttered. Finish with a coat of varnish to protect.

MATERIALS

White acrylic primer

Coloured emulsion paint – base coat

Coloured emulsion paint – for tartan

Fine artists' brushes

Polyurethane varnish

FURNITURE FACELIFTS

TARTAN TALLBOY

1 First, prepare the tallboy by sanding down and applying the primer, then coat with two layers of coloured emulsion base coat. Mark out your first lines with a pencil and ruler, this will give you an accurate a start as possible. Draw four lines in sets of two with a 2.5cm/1in gap between each set, and then leave a 15cm/1in space before the next four lines. Repeat this pattern using different colours for the vertical and horizontal lines.

MATERIALS

White acrylic primer

Coloured emulsion paint – base coat

5 coloured emulsion paints – for tartan effect

Fine artists' brushes

Pencil

Masking tape

Sandpaper

Ruler

2 With a third colour, draw a tightly packed trio of lines through the middle of the 15cm/6in gap. It looks effective if you paint a thick line through the centre and a thinner line on either side. Work on the horizontal first and then repeat the process, using a slightly darker colour, along the vertical. By now, you may be feeling more confident drawing the lines freehand and it certainly doesn't matter if the lines are wobbly, as this simply adds to the appeal.

3 This is an extremely colourful project, so make sure that you allow a colour to dry completely before applying the next to avoid them running into each other. The fifth and final colour should be the boldest, adding a dramatic finishing touch to your design. Position these lines within the 2.5cm/1in gap running between the original vertical and horizontal lines.

HINT

It will, of course, be impossible to paint the cupboard as a whole as you will not be able to achieve straight lines in this way, however if you break it down into sections – a drawer at a time for example, it will not seem so daunting.

FURNITURE **FACELIFTS**

GLOSSARY OF TERMS

Acetate sheet
A synthetic material made from cellulose acetate, which makes an excellent stencil. It is durable, easy to clean and transparent – meaning designs can be traced or drawn directly onto the surface and then cut out with a craft knife.

Antiquing wax
Seals and protects surfaces in the same way as ordinary wax but has a slightly different finish that gives the appearance of age.

Baste
The term used when fabric is sewn together with very loose or temporary stitches.

Crackle glaze
This is applied to a surface, left to dry and then painted over with a layer of emulsion. As the emulsion begins to interact with the glaze it forms cracks, creating a distressed or antique appearance.

Dutch metal leaf
This can be used instead of gold leaf. It is a cheaper alternative and is sold in a versatile sheet form so is easy to use. The only slight disadvantage is that unlike gold leaf, Dutch leaf must be varnished.

Emulsion paint
Used in the majority of painted projects featured in this book, emulsion is the broad term used for water-based paints that contain vinyl or acrylic resins.

Fusible webbing
A soft material that glues two pieces of fabric together once pressed with a hot iron, which activates an adhesive. It can be used as an alternative to sewing but you should be aware that it is not as durable as needle and thread.

Masking fluid
Similar to masking tape in the way that it will not allow paints or stains to soak through onto the surface that you are working on. The difference is that masking fluid comes in liquid form and is applied with a brush. Once dry, it forms a rubbery protective layer, which can be painted over and later peeled off.

Manilla card
This is a tough, traditional stencilling sheet. It is made by soaking card in linseed oil to make it strong and water-resistant. It can be wiped clean, and easily cut with a craft knife but unlike acetate, it is not transparent.

Paint kettle
This is the common name for any container in which paints are mixed. Normally made of metal or plastic, they are essential for achieving the perfect colour, and should be cleaned well after each use.

Primer

After wood has been sanded down, primer is applied to seal the surface and prevent any paint from soaking in. It provides an excellent base for the finish coats and is available in water-based, oil-based and acrylic varieties.

Registration marks

If you are using a stencil with one or more transparent overlays you will need to make registration marks on each sheet for accurate alignment of the stencil.

Repositioning spray

A temporary fixing agent that is sprayed onto the back of a stencil to hold a design in place and prevent paint from seeping under the bridges of the stencil. It can be lifted and repositioned several times before further application is necessary, and does not leave traces of adhesive.

Sanding block

This consists of a piece of sandpaper wrapped around a block of wood. It is most useful when sanding large objects because it is easier to grip than just a single sheet of sandpaper.

Self-adhesive plastic

A transparent, adhesive material, similar to sellotape, but consisting of a non-adhesive backing sheet. It can be cut into any shape and is useful for masking off areas of an object that you don't wish to paint. It can be applied to most surfaces and peeled off without tearing or causing damage.

Template

The term used for a pattern or design, normally cut from metal, wood or thick cardboard, which is used to draw around in order to reproduce identical shapes quickly and accurately.

Transfer paper

This works in a similar way to carbon copy paper. A design, which has been reproduced onto tracing paper, is placed on top of a sheet of transfer paper and is outlined once more with pencil. The same image will be transferred through to the surface you are working on.

Wire wool

Available in fine, medium and coarse grades, this material scratches the surface of an object enabling it to hold paint better. It can also be used to remove patches of paint to create a distressed finish. It works in a very similar way to sandpaper.